Keltic Creatures

for Kids 2

Kathy O'Meara

Perelandra Design

This small (5x8) book contains 17 drawings of Keltic Creatures. These characters are geared to appeal to younger children.

Books by Kathy O'Meara

Keltic Crosses Coloring
Keltic Crosses Coloring 2
Keltic Alphabet Coloring: Capital Letters
Keltic Alphabet Coloring: Lower Case Letters
Keltic Coloring: Knots & Numbers
Keltic Coloring: Knotted Nature
Keltic Alphabet Coloring 2: Capital Letters
Keltic Alphabet Coloring 2: Lower Case Letters
Keltic Creatures For Kids
Keltic Creatures For Kids 2
Keltic Knots For Kids

Stained Glass "Window" Patterns

Spring Flowers
Summer Flowers
Autumn
Circle of Life
Keltic Christian

International Standard Book Number

ISBN-13: 978-1727274271
ISBN-10: 172727427X

KEESHOND

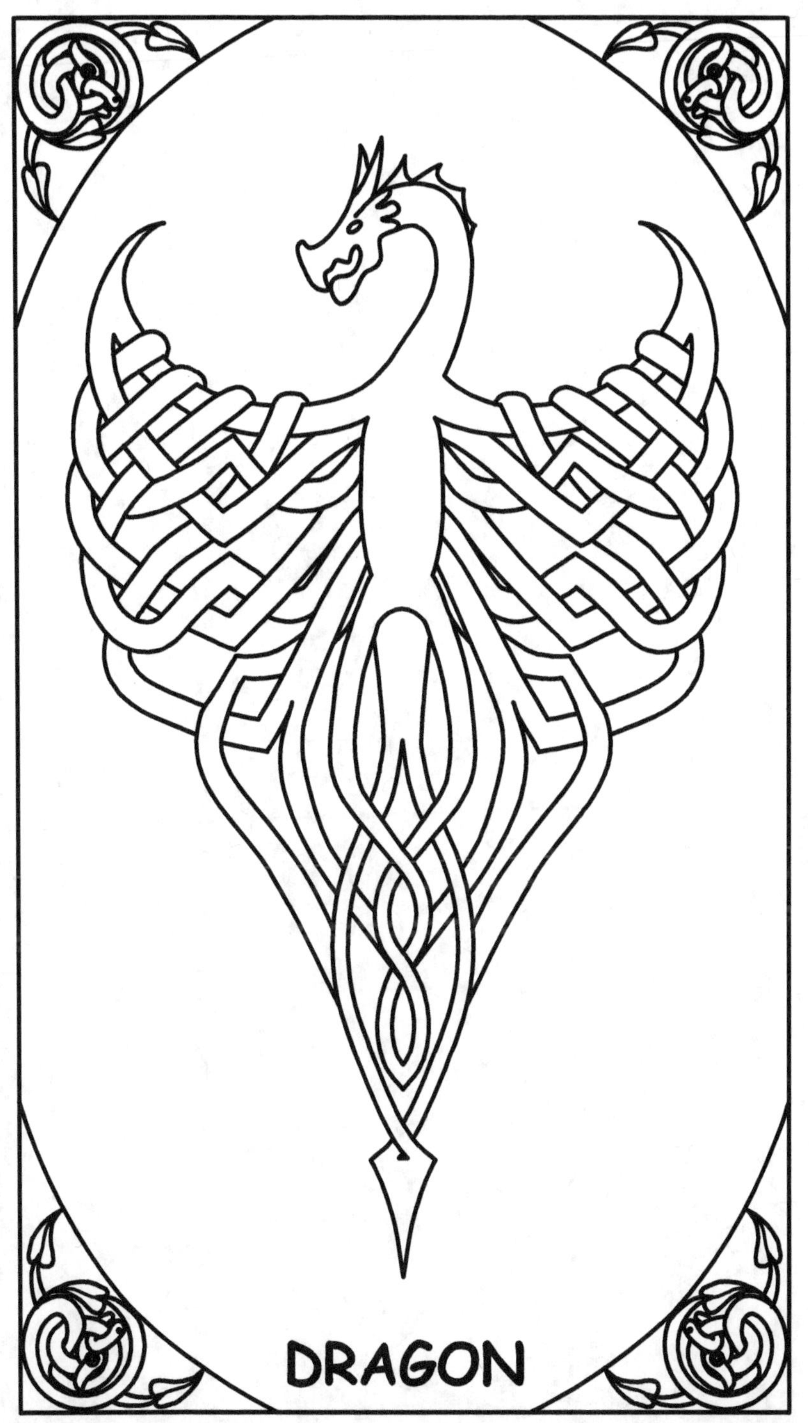

DRAGON

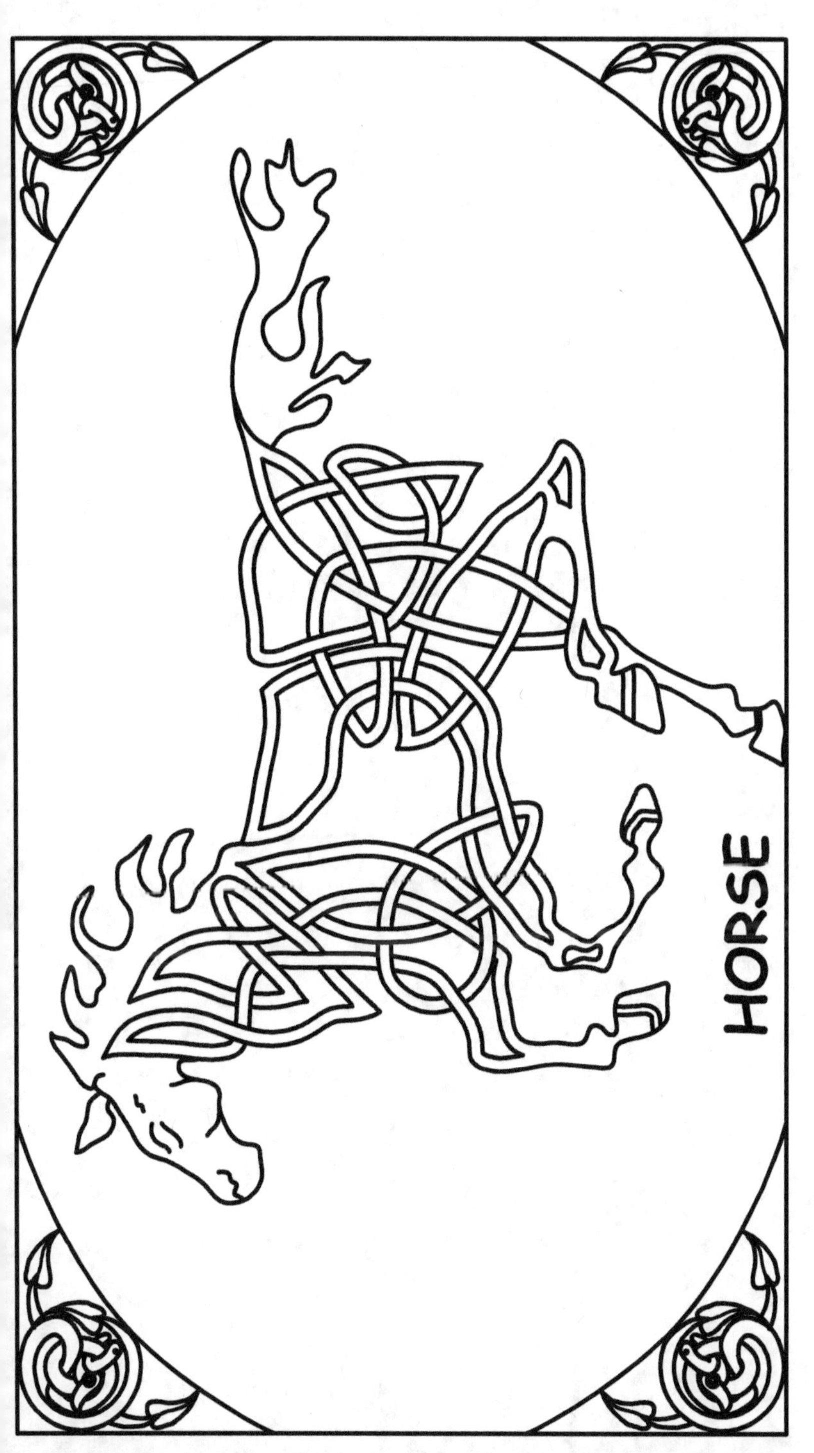
HORSE

OWL

BUTTERFLY

EAGLE

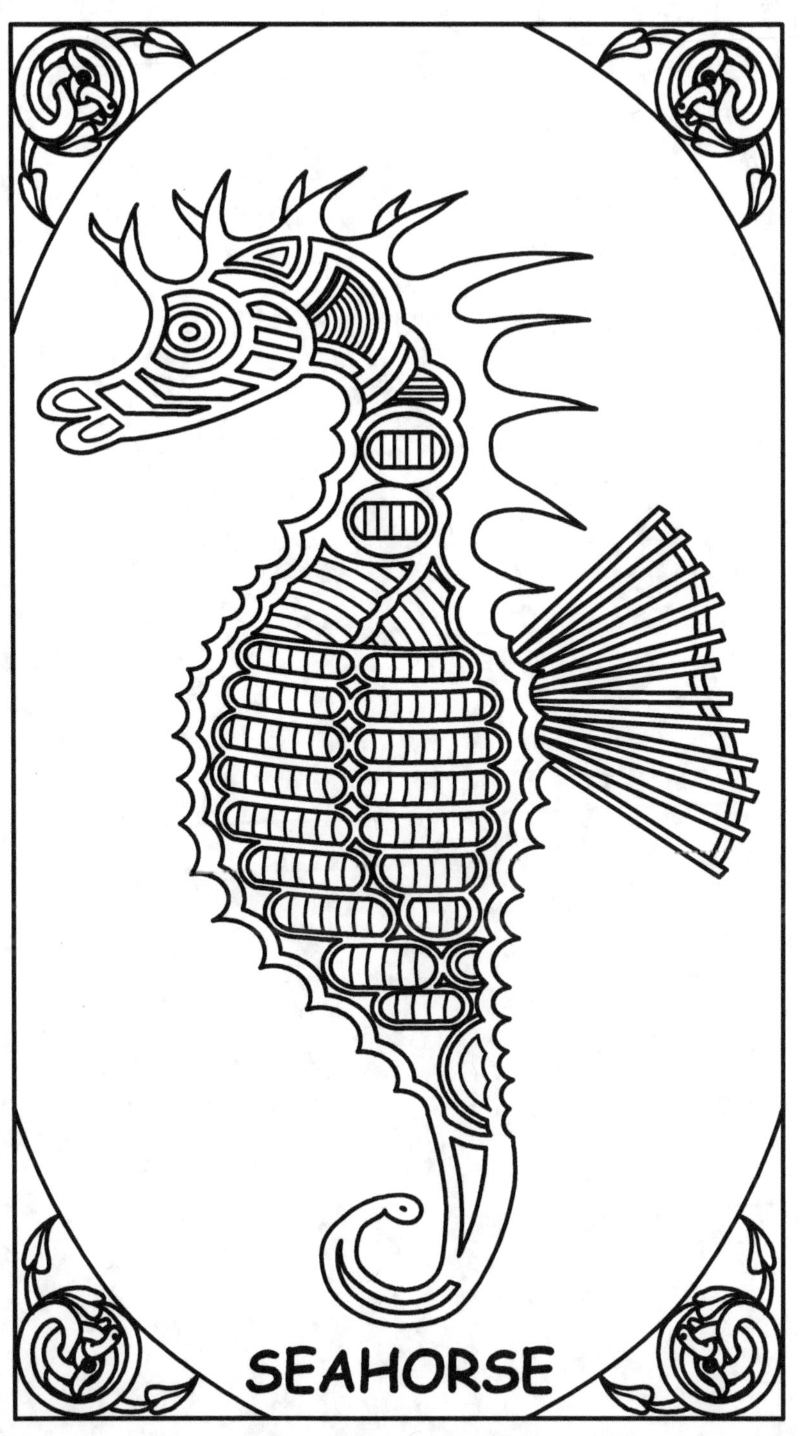

SEAHORSE

SWAN

JELLYFISH

4 DOGS

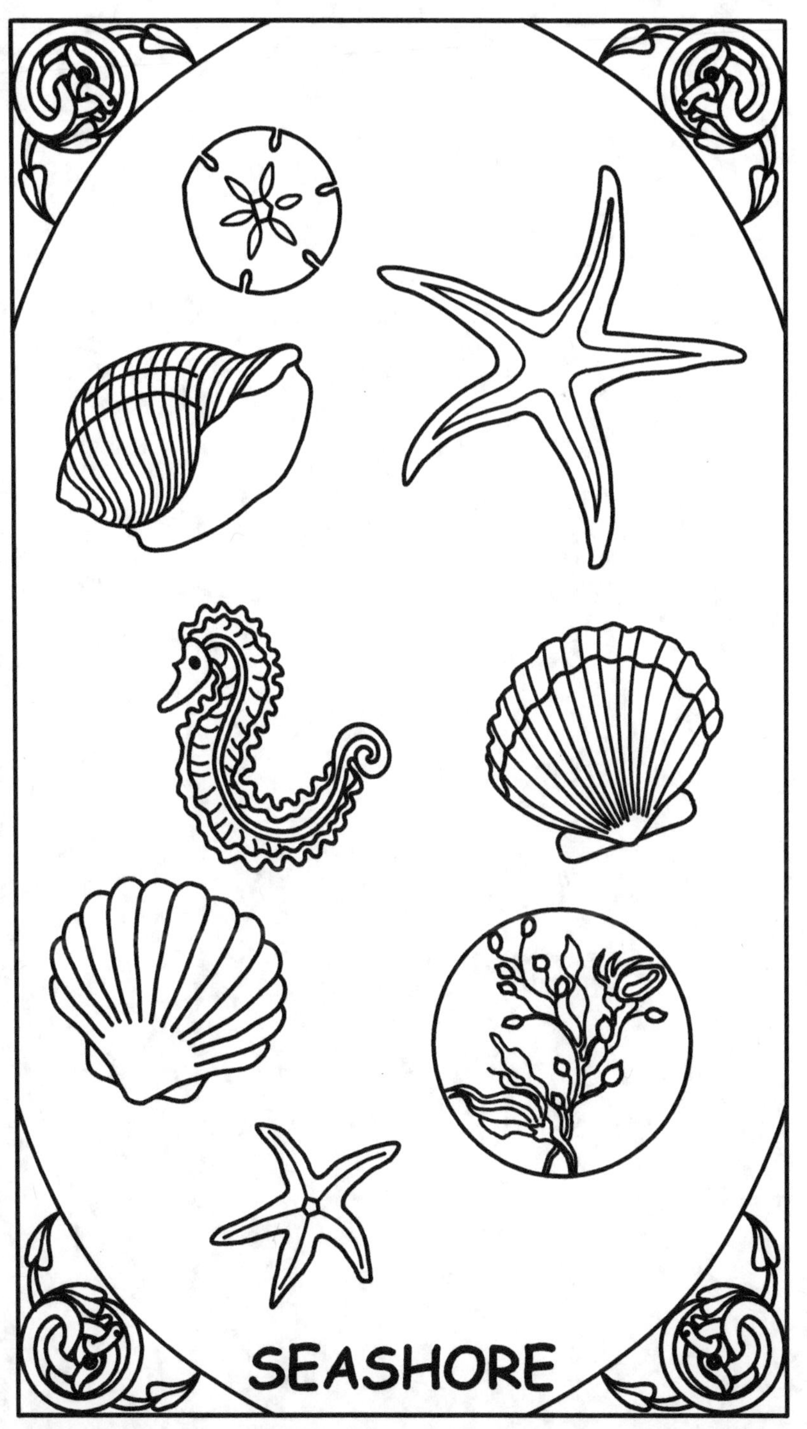

SEASHORE

DRAGON

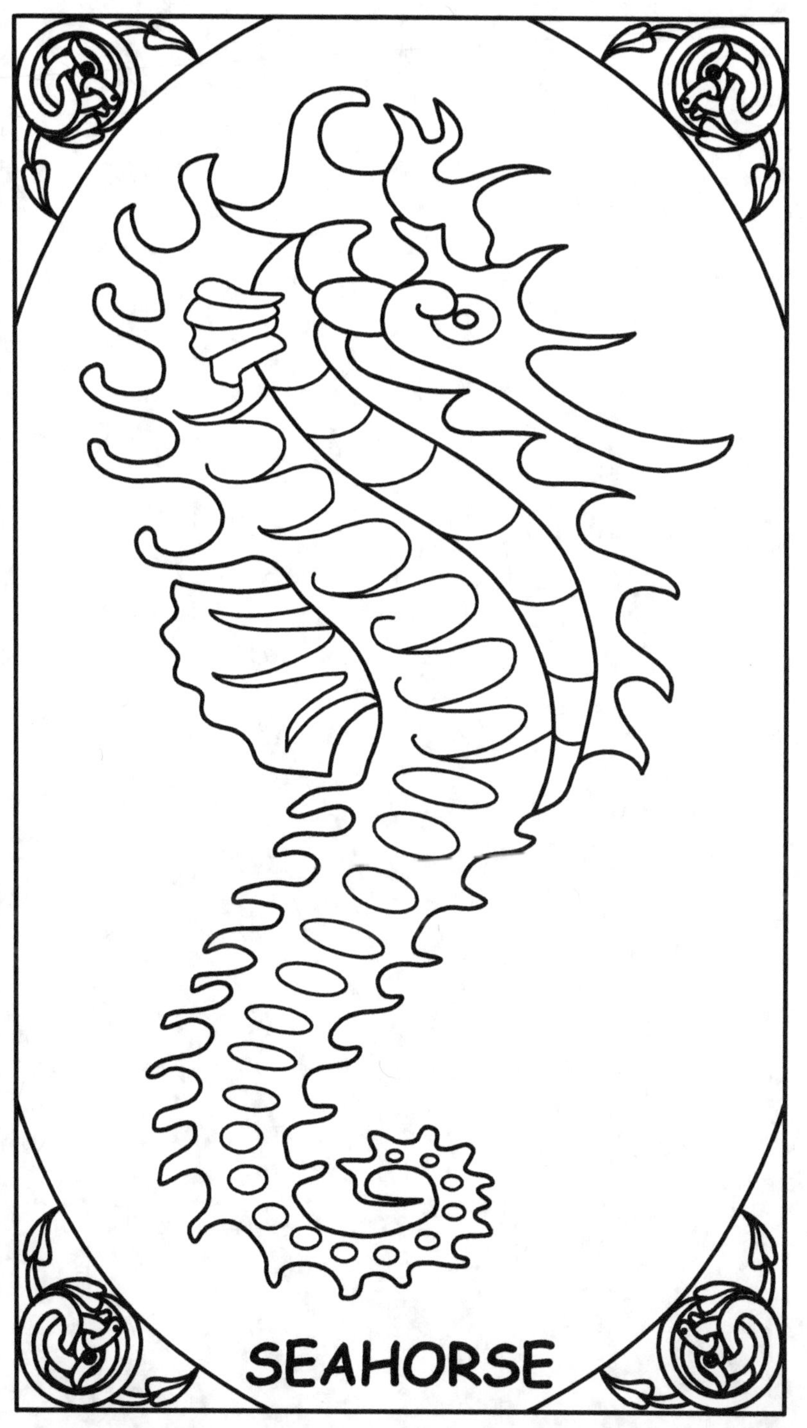

SEAHORSE

DRAGON

WOLF

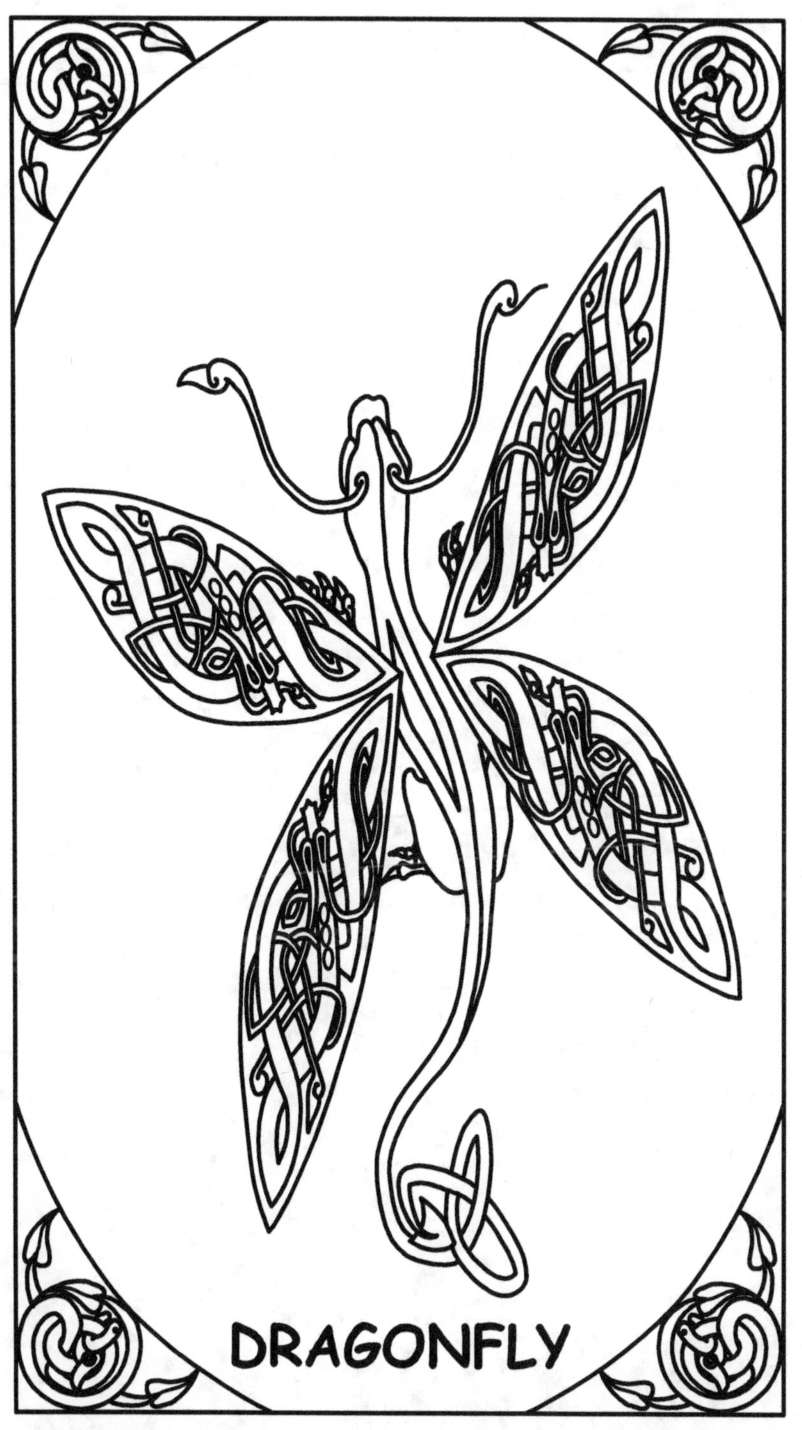

DRAGONFLY

OWL

DOVE

FISH